Girl, You Are Magic!

WRITTEN BY:
Ashley Aya Ferguson

ILLUSTRATED BY:
Lee Edmond Johnson

Manufactured in the United States of America
ISBN-13: 978-0-692-08557-8
ISBN-10: 0-692-08557-2

For Nia. Never forget that you are magic.

Girl, you are *magic!*

Do you know that you are magic?
Not in a spooky, witchy way.

But if you believe in yourself
you can make the impossible, possible –
Every single day.

Girl, you are *magic!*

Do you know you are magic?
Speak up, stand tall and take your place.

Someone out there needs you – yes you!
So don't get lost in space.

WHERE did you get this *magic?*

Well, inside of you! You just have to stir it up.

Shake it, wake it, but girl **DON'T BREAK IT**; you have just enough.

WHAT IS this *magic* stuff, you ask?
The rhythm in your walk,
the melody in your talk
and the charm in your smile.

YOU are treasured, a very important person.
YOU have value that lasts for miles.

Magic **girls just like you** changed the world's course!

Queens and revolutionaries went directly to the source.

Writers, scientists, athletes, performers; they did not ever quit.

Pick a challenge, pick a cause, pick a sport – **you already know you can conquer it!**

YOU'VE *got* **WHAT THEY HAVE**
and maybe even a little bit more.

Something you do might even be
better than all those things before.

And, when someone tries to tell you
that you cannot do it,

Make sure you tell them to have a seat
while they watch **you push right through it.**

And girl,

DON'T get discouraged.
If you're not the best at everything,
don't be sour.

You know even the best superheroes
typically only have one superpower.

Imagine **how boring life**
will be if you don't use your magic.

And think of all those sad people,
who all wish they had it.

You were born with gifts
that no one else can brag.

So be the best **YOU** and
don't try to copy anyone's swag.

Girl, you are more *magic*

than you even know.

Just look in the mirror at that

beautiful glow!

About The Author

Ashley Ferguson is the mother of one magical girl named Nia. She wrote this book so that Nia and other girls like her will always remember that they are magic. Ashley is an Ohio native and spends her days, evenings, mornings, nights and weekends with words.

Printed in the USA
CPSIA information can be obtained
at www.ICGtesting.com
LVHW071240141023
760671LV00026B/247